DAILY WISDOM

DAILYWISDOM

365 BUDDHIST INSPIRATIONS

edited by Josh Bartok

WISDOM PUBLICATIONS • BOSTON

Wisdom Publications
199 Elm Street
Somerville MA 02144 USA
www.wisdompubs.org

Library of Congress Cataloging-in-Publication Data

Daily wisdom: 365 Buddhist inspirations / edited by Josh Bartok.
    p. cm.
  Includes bibliographical references.
  ISBN 0-86171-300-1 (alk. paper)
  1. Buddhist devotional calendars. 2. Buddhist meditations.
  I. Bartok, Josh.
BQ5579.D35 2001
2001033333

06 05 04 03 02
6 5 4 3 2

Cover design by Laura Shaw Feit
Interior by Gopa and the Bear
Cover image courtesy of Photodisc.

Special thanks to Eveline Yang, whose assistance was of
inestimable value in the preparation of this work.

Wisdom Publications' books are printed on acid-free paper and
meet the guidelines for the permanence and durability set by
the Council on Library Resources.

Printed in Canada.

Dedicated

with boundless gratitude

to all our teachers

and to all beings.

PREFACE

Cited within these pages are representatives from many streams of Buddhist thought and practice: Tibetan lamas and Burmese teachers, Zen masters and tantric adepts, Asians and Westerners, monastics and lay people, poets and pundits. And yet, as diverse as these sources are, their words all point to the same open, compassionate heart and wise, unhindered mind.

Our utmost gratitude goes to the myriad teachers, translators, and editors whose generous efforts have given rise to the original works from which *Daily Wisdom* is drawn. We hope the page-a-day format invites you to spend a few moments of quiet reflection with each excerpt to truly feel the beating heart of these living words. But most of all, in offering this compilation it is our sincere hope that you find encouragement, illumination, perhaps even solace, as you follow your own path deeper into daily wisdom.

Josh Bartok
on behalf of the staff of
Wisdom Publications
Somerville, Mass.

"How, dear sir, did you cross the flood?"

"By not halting, friend, and by not straining I crossed the flood."

"But how is it, dear sir, that by not halting and by not straining you crossed the flood?"

"When I came to a standstill, friend, then I sank; but when I struggled, then I got swept away. It is in this way, friend, that by not halting and by not straining I crossed the flood."

There simply is nothing to which we can attach ourselves, no matter how hard we try. In time, things will change and the conditions that produced our current desires will be gone. Why then cling to them now?

The temptation is to conclude that perhaps meditation is alright for some but dead wrong for you. In my case, meditation started out painful and tedious beyond words. Extremely convincing arguments for giving up before you have even started will almost certainly occur to you— don't listen to them.

When we fall on the ground it hurts us, but we also need to rely on the ground to get back up.

Wisdom does not mean knowledge but experiential understanding. Wisdom helps you to change radically your habits and perceptions, as you discover the constantly changing, interconnected nature of the whole of existence.

JANUARY 6

We plant merit with our minds, and we commit crimes with our minds. With our minds, we imprint images. This one mind is like an artist. It can draw anything, and what it draws is realized. If you surrender your impressions, ideas, thoughts, and so on at the moment they arise without imprinting them on your mind, your mind will not be tainted, just as the lotus flower is not tainted by the muddy water whence it grows.

This mind and body is our household. If this inner household is not in order, no outer household can be in order.

No matter how hard you pursue pleasure and success, there are times when you fail. No matter how fast you flee, there are times when pain catches up with you.

Try to be reasonable in the way you grow, and don't ever think it is too late. It is never too late. Even if you are going to die tomorrow, keep yourself straight and clear and be a happy human being today. If you keep your situation happy day by day, you will eventually reach the greatest happiness of enlightenment.

On the basis of the belief that all human beings share the same divine nature, we have a very strong ground, a very powerful reason, to believe that it is possible for each of us to develop a genuine sense of equanimity toward all beings.

Honesty can be cultivated by transforming your inner language. For example, you might think: "I am no good" or "They are not good." Is this true? For some strange reason, people want to wallow in the idea of being either the best or the worst. What is true in this moment? How close can we get to the reality of our experiences?

The present moment is changing so fast that we often do not notice its existence at all. Every moment of mind is like a series of pictures passing though a projector. Some of the pictures come from sense impressions. Others come from memories of past experiences or from fantasies of the future. Mindfulness helps us freeze the frame so that we can become aware of our sensations and experiences as they are, without the distorting coloration of socially conditioned responses or habitual reactions.

Leave the mind in its natural, undisturbed state.
Don't follow thoughts of "This is a problem, that is a
problem!" Without labeling difficulties as problems,
leave your mind in its natural state. In this way,
you will stop seeing miserable conditions as problems.

JANUARY 14

There is a well-known simile about a monkey trap of the kind used in Asia—a wooden container with a small opening. Inside lies a sweet. The monkey, attracted by the sweet, puts his paw into the opening and grasps the sweet. When he wants to draw his paw out again, he cannot get his fist with the sweet through the narrow opening. He is trapped until the hunter comes and captures him. He does not realize that all he has to do to be free is let go of the sweet. That is the way we live our lives. We are trapped because we want it nice and sweet. Not being able to let go, we are caught in the never-ending cycle of happiness and unhappiness, hope and despair.

Baizhang asked, "What is the essential import of the school?"
Mazu said, "It's just the place where you let go of your body
  and life."

All the faults of our mind—our selfishness, ignorance, anger, attachment, guilt, and other disturbing thoughts—are temporary, not permanent and everlasting. And since the cause of our suffering—our disturbing thoughts and obscurations—is temporary, our suffering is also temporary.

It's not enough just to sit down and then, with a totally mundane motivation, proceed into meditation. Rather, among the possibilities of having a virtuous, nonvirtuous, or ethically neutral motivation, it is necessary to bring forth a virtuous motivation, specifically the spirit of awakening for the sake of all sentient beings.

Just as a monkey roaming through a forest grabs hold of one branch, lets that go and grabs another, then lets that go and grabs still another, so too that which is called "mind" and "mentality" and "consciousness" arises as one thing and ceases as another by day and by night.

Remember, lifelong habits die hard. It is difficult enough to simply recognize our anger and jealousy, let alone to make an effort to hold back the old familiar tide of feeling or analyze its cause and results. Transforming the mind is a slow and gradual process. It is a matter of ridding ourselves, bit by bit, of instinctive, harmful habit patterns and becoming familiar with habits that necessarily bring positive results—to ourselves and others.

Zen teachers talk quite often about how you will make compromises when you try to practice on your own. As you are not disturbing anyone else, you don't mind shifting position to get a bit more comfortable—and then shifting again. You may cut the sitting short, then a bit shorter—then end up not sitting at all. But it is your own sitting that you disturb by moving, destroying the effort you've made up until then, by stirring up the mind and the ego. It is yourself that you cheat.

If we divide into two camps—even into the violent and the nonviolent—and stand in one camp while attacking the other, the world will never have peace. We will always blame and condemn those we feel are responsible for wars and social injustice, without recognizing the degree of violence in ourselves. We must work on ourselves and also with those we condemn if we want to have a real impact.

Those who merely read books cannot understand the teachings and, what's more, may even go astray. But those who try to observe the things going on in the mind, and always take that which is true in their own minds as their standard, never get muddled. They are able to comprehend suffering, and ultimately will understand Dharma. Then, they will understand the books they read.

If you never try, you can never be successful; but if you try, you might surprise yourself.

The purpose of all the major religious traditions is not to construct big temples on the outside, but to create temples of goodness and compassion *inside*, in our hearts.

There's but little breath left
on the boundary of this life and next.
Not knowing if I'll be here next morning,
why try to trick death
with life-schemes for a permanent future?

You can expect certain benefits from meditation. The initial ones are practical things; the later stages are profoundly transcendental. They run together from the simple to the sublime.

Pulling up
My robes, I draw magic water
From the spring and let it surge,
To scrub clogs and headcloth. Smoky
Haze breaking over fir and bamboo,
Clears and concentrates
The mind and spirit.

And what is the wholesome? Abstention from killing living
beings is wholesome; abstention from taking what is not given
is wholesome; abstention from misconduct in sensual pleasures
is wholesome; abstention from false speech is wholesome;
abstention from malicious speech is wholesome; abstention from
harsh speech is wholesome; abstention from gossip is wholesome;
uncovetousness is wholesome; non-ill will is wholesome; right
view is wholesome. This is called the wholesome.

And what is the root of the wholesome? Non-greed is a root
of the wholesome; non-hate is a root of the wholesome;
non-delusion is a root of the wholesome. This is called the
root of the wholesome.

Thinking of human beings alone is a bit narrow. To consider that all sentient beings in the universe have been our mother at some point in time opens a space of compassion.

By renouncing samsara, we renounce our habitual grasping, unhappy minds. And by renouncing samsara, we embrace our potential for enlightenment.

JANUARY 31

It is crucial to know when it is appropriate to withdraw our attention from things that disturb our mind. However, if the only way we know how to deal with certain objects is to avoid them, there will be a severe limit as to how far our spiritual practice can take us.

When non-action is realized, it is the true nature.
There is no other buddha outside of that.

In the unthinkable, inscrutable, ordinary nature of reality there is no difference between freedom and bondage. No matter what arises, when you perceive your original nature, the joy arises automatically—and what joy!

Fame is the flattery of Mara.

ADEPT GODRAKPA, IN *HERMIT OF GO CLIFFS*

We walk on frosted ground
praising chrysanthemums bordering fields;
sit on the east edge of the woods
waiting for the moon to rise.
Not having to be alone
is happiness;
we do not talk
of failure or success.

Do not cling to any one thing. Nothing is it, so do not judge and criticize. No intellectual concepts are valid, so do not presume.

The greater our awareness regarding the value and effectiveness of other religious traditions, then the deeper will be our respect and reverence toward other religions. This is the proper way for us to promote genuine compassion and a spirit of harmony among the religions of the world.

Even a strong wind is empty by nature.
Even a great wave is just ocean itself.
Even thick southern clouds are insubstantial as sky.
Even the dense mind is naturally birthless.

Since the old days, it is said that "anger is the fire in one's mind that burns away all of one's virtuous deeds." Anger should be absolutely surrendered.

According to the Buddha, our minds are naturally luminous. In each moment, as consciousness first arises, its spark is bright. In the unenlightened mind, however, that spark gets covered up by the impurities of greed, hatred, and delusion. These impurities obstruct the mind's brightness, leaving the mind dark and miserable.

Greed is an imperfection that defiles the mind; hate is an imperfection that defiles the mind; delusion is an imperfection that defiles the mind.

Wisdom has three stages. The first one is knowledge acquired by hearing or reading. We reach the second stage when we make this knowledge our own by taking its guidelines to heart and trying to actualize them through thought, speech, and action. As we do this more and more, our thoughts, words, and deeds are purified, and the third and highest stage of wisdom arises.

After becoming an abbot, Yunyan addressed the monks,
   saying, "There is the son of a certain household. There is no
   question that he can't answer."
Dongshan came forward and asked, "How many classic books
   are there in his house?"
Yunyan said, "Not a single word."
Dongshan said, "Then how can he be so knowledgeable?"
Yunyan said, "Day and night he has never slept."
Dongshan said, "Can he be asked about a certain matter?"
Yunyan said, "What he answers is not spoken."

Beings who perceive what can be expressed
Become established in what can be expressed.
Not fully understanding what can be expressed,
They come under the yoke of Death.
But having fully understood what can be expressed,
One does not conceive "one who expresses."
For that does not exist for him
By which one could describe him.

BUDDHA, IN *THE CONNECTED DISCOURSES OF THE BUDDHA*

It is precisely because our present life is so inseparably linked with desire that we must make use of desire's tremendous energy if we wish to transform our life into something transcendental.

The Buddha could accomplish the enlightened mind because its very nature was already there. That is why buddhahood—enlightenment—is possible. If there were no such nature or potential, it would be impossible.

You can only have bliss if you don't chase it.

This fundamental consciousness
In itself is nothing at all.
In the voidness of reality
Lack of realizer and realized is realized,
Lack of seer and seen is seen,
Lack of knower and known is known,
Lack of perceiver and perceived is perceived.

FEBRUARY 18

Unless we practice loving feelings toward everyone we meet, day in, day out, we're missing out on the most joyous part of life. If we can actually open our hearts, there's no difficulty in being happy.

A monk asked Shigui, "What is the first principle?"
Shigui said, "What you just asked is the second principle."

In order to train in the path that would allow us to transform death, the intermediate state, and rebirth, we have to practice on three occasions: during the waking state, during the sleeping state, and during the process of death.

Don't forget to bring the good experiences of meditation into your daily activities. Instead of acting and reacting impulsively and following your thoughts and feelings here and there, watch your mind carefully, be aware, and try to deal skillfully with problems as they arise. If you can do this each day, your meditation will have been successful.

So many of our problems arise because we always feel cut off from something we need. We do not feel whole and therefore turn expectantly toward other people for the qualities we imagine missing in ourselves. All of the problems of the world, from one person's anxiety to warfare between nations, can be traced to this feeling of not being whole.

Your own practice can show you the truth. Your own experience is all that counts.

What does the spring wind have in mind,
Coming day and night to these groves and gardens?
It never asks who owns the peach and damson trees
But blows away their crimson without a word.

FEBRUARY 25

Looking for *it*, the vision cannot be seen: cease your search.
It cannot be discovered through meditation, so abandon your
trance states and mental images. *It* cannot be accomplished by
anything you do, so give up the attempt to treat the world as
magical illusion. *It* cannot be found by seeking, so abandon all
hope of results.

FEBRUARY 26

Attachment is the mind stuck to an object.

If we pick up the handle, we pick up the pot. Similarly, if we meditate on and develop compassion—the wish that all others be without suffering—we hold within us the essence of all other Dharma practices.

GESHE NGAWANG DHARGYEY, IN *ADVICE FROM A SPIRITUAL FRIEND*

The more compassionate you are, the more generous you can be. The more generous you are, the more loving-friendliness you cultivate to help the world.

Trust has nothing to do with moral courage. It occurs when we have nowhere else to turn, when we reach the end of our need to control.

MARCH 1

Whenever you hear that someone else has been successful, rejoice. Always practice rejoicing for others—whether your friend or your enemy. If you cannot practice rejoicing, no matter how long you live, you will not be happy.

Having enjoyed a sweet delicious taste,
And having sometimes tasted what is bitter,
Do not greedily enjoy the sweet taste,
Do not feel aversion toward the bitter.

When touched by pleasant contact, do not be enthralled,
Do not tremble when touched by pain.
Look evenly on both the pleasant and painful,
Not drawn or repelled by anything.

MARCH 3

Explaining many profound dharmas is easy;
living them yourself is hard.

Some dubious people with little real spiritual training call themselves teachers, but actually take advantage of others in the name of taking care of peace of mind. This is unfortunate. It happens because, when it comes to spirituality, people are still very gullible.

Whatever is not yours, abandon it. When you have abandoned it, that will lead to your welfare and happiness.

Everything is mind-made.

When I received the news of cancer, I understood, Oh, yes, what is required of me now is that I be fully present to each new experience as it comes and that I engage with it as completely as I can. I don't mean that I said this to myself. Nothing so conscious as that. I mean that my whole being turned, and looked, and moved toward the experience.

Enlightenment—that magnificent escape from anguish and ignorance—never happens by accident. It results from the brave and sometimes lonely battle of one person against his own weaknesses.

Nothing worthwhile is achieved overnight.

MOURNING THE DEATH
OF CH'AN MASTER PO-YEN

Fresh moss covers
the stone bed;
how many springtimes
was it the Master's?

His profile in meditation
has been sketched;
but the body of the meditator
has been burned.

Snow in the pines
has closed the pagoda courtyard;
dust settles in the lock
on the sutra library.

I chide myself
for these two tears—
a man who hasn't grasped
the empty nature of all things.

MARCH 11

The Buddha compared people to four kinds of clay vessels.
One type of vessel has holes in the bottom. We can pour in as
much water as we like and it runs right out. When this type of
person hears the Dharma, it goes in one ear and out the other.
The second type of vessel has cracks. Though we pour in the
Dharma, it seeps out slowly until the vessel is empty again.
The third vessel is full to the brim with stale water—views and
opinions. One can't pour anything new in, everything is
already known. The only useful vessel is the fourth, without
holes or cracks and totally empty.

A monk asked, "When the great matter of life and
    death arrives, then what?"
Dasui said, "If there's tea, drink tea. If there's food, eat food."
The monk said, "Who receives this support?"
Dasui said, "Just pick up your bowl."

MARCH 13

Often, new meditators think that their negative minds are getting worse, not better! And they feel that it is meditation that has caused it. Consider what happens when you wash clothes. When you first put them into water, a certain amount of dirt comes out. As you continue to scrub them the water becomes dirtier and dirtier. It would be foolish to blame the soap, water, and scrubbing for the dirt—the process of washing merely reveals what is there already and is the right method for completely removing the dirt. Similarly, meditation is the way to purify the mind of what is already there: at first we discover the gross negativities, and then the more subtle. So be patient, and don't worry!

One who seeks delight in form seeks delight in suffering. One who seeks delight in suffering, I say, is not freed from suffering.

BUDDHA, IN *THE CONNECTED DISCOURSES OF THE BUDDHA*

MARCH 15

Share your love, your wisdom, and your wealth and serve each other as much as possible. Live in harmony with one another and be an example of peace, love, compassion, and wisdom. Try to be happy in your practice, to be satisfied with your life. Be reasonable in the way you grow, and don't ever think that it is too late. And don't be afraid of death. Even if you are going to die tomorrow, at least for today keep yourself straight and clean-clear, and be a happy human being.

MARCH 16

Buddha is no longer Buddha when you enclose him in your mind—Buddha becomes only your mind's discriminative notion.

MARCH 17

Body impermanent like spring mist;
mind insubstantial like empty sky;
thoughts unestablished like breezes in space.
Think about these three points over and over.

Emptiness is not a negative state; it denotes a mind that has no tension, no worry or fear, and is wide open to see the Dharma within. Such a mind has let go of all preconceived ideas about the world and the people in it. If our ideas up to now have not brought total and absolute happiness, it is much better to let go of them and be an empty vessel into which the Dharma can be poured. As the Dharma fills us, it changes our outlook and eventually brings us to right view.

The you that goes in one side of the meditation experience is not the same you that comes out the other side.

MARCH 20

The more we reflect on old age and death, the more we see it as a natural process. It is nothing extraordinary. If we prepare ourselves in this way, then when such events actually happen, the work of accepting them as a very normal part of our life is already done. We can simply think, "Now is the period where my life's end is coming." I think that is a better approach.

Mountain sounds carry a chill wisdom,
an upwelling spring whispers subtle tales,
pine breezes stir the fire beneath my tea,
bamboo shadows soak deep into my robe.

I grind my ink: clouds scraping across the crags
copy out a verse: birds settling on branches
as the world rolls right on by
its every turn tracing out non-action.

MARCH 22

We cannot hope to attain our goal of universal and complete happiness by systematically making ourselves more and more miserable. This is contrary to the way things actually work. It is only by cultivating small experiences of calm and satisfaction now that we will be able to achieve our ultimate goal of peace and tranquility in the future.

LAMA THUBTEN YESHE, *INTRODUCTION TO TANTRA*

Realize that the journey to the center takes place within your own mind.

MORNING TRAVEL

Rising early
to begin the journey;
not a sound
from the chickens next door.

Beneath the lamp,
I part from the innkeeper;
on the road, my skinny horse
moves through the dark.

Slipping on stones
newly frosted,
threading through woods,
we scare up birds roosting.

After a bell tolls
far in the mountains,
the colors of daybreak
gradually clear.

We should not merely expend all our energy collecting pieces of information, but make an effort to experience their validity through insight in our daily life.

Toss to the winds your concern for this life,
and impress on your mind the unknown time of your death.
Remembering the pain of samsara,
why long for the unnecessary?

MILAREPA, *DRINKING THE MOUNTAIN STREAM*

The essential truth of suffering is that neither individual nor social problems are due chiefly to external conditions.

If we can reach the understanding of what we actually are, there is no better remedy for eliminating all suffering. This is the heart of all spiritual practices.

We are not compelled to meditate by some outside agent, by other people, or by God. Rather, just as we are responsible for our own suffering, so are we solely responsible for our own cure. We have created the situation in which we find ourselves, and it is up to us to create the circumstances for our release.

In meditation, don't expect anything. Just sit back and see what happens. Treat the whole thing as an experiment. Take an active interest in the test itself, but don't get distracted by your expectations about the results. For that matter, don't be anxious for any result whatsoever.

MARCH 31

A monk asked, "What is Buddha?"
Chongshou said, "What is Buddha?"
The monk asked, "What is understanding?"
Chongshou said, "Understanding is not understanding."

APRIL 1

You follow desire, and you are not satisfied.
Again you follow desire, and again you are not satisfied.
Again you try, and again you are not satisfied.

APRIL 2

Not recognizing that there's no connection
between term and meaning
those who wander in endless jargon
get so exhausted.

The only foundation stone of practice is renunciation.
The only gateway of practice is faith.
The only approach to practice is compassion.

APRIL 4

In the eating hall, a stuffed parrot hung from the ceiling, and from its golden beak dangled a card that read, "We are in training to be nobody special." I had often repeated this to myself, working against my need for achievement and recognition, and the discontent that could engender. "I am in training to be nobody special." Saying the words in my mind, I felt how they redirected me from a certain seductive struggle and excitement and disease, into a more stable focus: forget what others think of you, forget the future goal of achievement; arrive instead in this body/mind, attending to this present moment. This is the whole of practice.

Some people live closely guarded lives, fearful of encountering someone or something that might shatter their insecure spiritual foundation. This attitude, however, is not the fault of religion but of their own limited understanding. True Dharma leads in exactly the opposite direction. It enables one to integrate all the many diverse experiences of life into a meaningful and coherent whole, thereby banishing fear and insecurity completely.

LAMA THUBTEN YESHE, IN *WISDOM ENERGY*

Don't strain. Don't force anything or make grand, exaggerated efforts. Meditation is not aggressive. There is no place or need for violent striving. Just let your effort be relaxed and steady.

Insofar as we all run from suffering
even experienced within a dream,
and yet always fall short of satisfaction
even within the heights of sublime happiness,
living beings cannot be differentiated.
It is therefore great self-delusion
to have no thought for the happiness of others.

APRIL 8

Our first priority should be to prepare a long-term strategy for improving the state of the world that focuses on the coming generations.

APRIL 9

The greatest support we can have is mindfulness, which means being totally present in each moment. If the mind remains centered, it cannot make up stories about the injustice of the world or one's friends, or about one's desires or sorrows. All these stories could fill many volumes, but when we are mindful such verbalizations stop. Being mindful means being fully absorbed in the moment, leaving no room for anything else. We are filled with the momentary happening, whatever it is—standing or sitting or lying down, feeling pleasure or pain—and we maintain a nonjudgmental awareness, a "just knowing."

Do not underestimate your ability.

APRIL 11

Who wrote this play in which we have to laugh, cry, and exit according to the script? No god can write it, nor can Buddha. Only your own mind can write it.

APRIL 12

Contrary to what some people might believe, there is nothing wrong with having pleasures and enjoyments. What is wrong is the confused way we grasp onto these pleasures, turning them from a source of happiness into a source of pain and dissatisfaction.

The more you practice the three trainings of ethics, meditation, and wisdom, the more difficult it will become for you to act in a way that is contrary to an ethical, compassionate attitude. Ethics arise naturally out of contemplating the three trainings.

Passing by the grieving temple,
the tiger
hears the sutra,
weeps.

We believe we own our thoughts and have to do something about them, especially if they are negative. This is bound to create suffering.

APRIL 16

A man named Liu Shiyu asked Yangshan, "May I hear the principle of attaining mind?"

Yangshan said, "If you want to attain mind, then there's no mind that can be attained. It is this unattainable mind that is known as truth."

Karma is not something complicated or philosophical. Karma means watching your body, watching your mouth, and watching your mind. Trying to keep these three doors as pure as possible is the practice of karma.

APRIL 18

It is not that anger and desire are inherently evil or that we should feel ashamed when they arise. It is a matter of seeing them as the delusions that they are: distorted conceptions that paint a false picture of reality. They are negative because they lead to unhappiness and confusion.

When you try to get rid of fear or anger, what happens? You just get restless or discouraged and have to go eat something or smoke or drink or do something else. But if you wait and endure restlessness, greed, hatred, doubt, despair, and sleepiness, if you observe these conditions as they cease and end, you will attain a kind of calm and mental clarity, which you will never achieve if you're always going after something else.

AJAHN SUMEDHO, *THE MIND AND THE WAY*

APRIL 20

It is said that there are only two tragedies in life:
not getting what one wants, and getting it.

All the wealth you've acquired
from beginningless time until now
has failed to fulfill all your desires.
Cultivate therefore this wish-granting gem
of moderation, O fortunate ones.

Realizing for ourselves that the power to achieve contentment comes from within requires an understanding of how our thinking process controls our behaviors and, thereby, our results.

APRIL 23

On one occasion the Blessed One was dwelling at Rajagaha in
the Maddakucchi Deer Park. Now on that occasion the Blessed
One's foot had been cut by a stone splinter. Severe pains assailed
the Blessed One—bodily feelings that were painful, racking,
sharp, piercing, harrowing, disagreeable. But the Blessed One
endured them, mindful and clearly comprehending, without
becoming distressed. Then the Blessed One had his outer robe
folded in four, and he lay down on his right side in the lion
posture with one leg overlapping the other, mindful and clearly
comprehending.

At the time of death, the best parting gift is peace of mind.

Imagine yourself as a child lying on your back, gazing up into a cloudless sky, and blowing soap bubbles through a plastic ring. As a bubble drifts up into the sky, you watch it rise, and this brings your attention into the sky. While you are looking at the bubble, it pops, and you keep your attention right where the bubble had been. Your awareness now lies in empty space.

APRIL 26

What is the skillful approach of someone seriously interested in realizing his or her highest potential? Stated simply, it is to keep the mind continuously in as happy and peaceful a condition as possible.

ABODE OF THE UNPLANNED EFFECT

The grass-covered path
is secluded and still;
a closed door faces
the Chungnan Mountains.

In the evening, the air's chilly,
but the light rain stops;
at dawn, far off,
a few cicadas start.

Leaves fall
where no green earth remains;
a person at his ease,
wears a plain, white robe.

With simplicity and plainness
his original nature still,
what need to practice
"calming of the heart"?

There is no pleasure without some degree of pain.
There is no pain without some amount of pleasure.

Do not wish for gratitude.

APRIL 30

Suppose, for example, that a worried miser carries everywhere with him a bag of money, nervously guarding it, refusing to open it and spend any of it; and then someone comes and persuades him to open the bag to the light of day, revealing that it now holds nothing but chewed paper and a dead rat. Would not the owner at once drop the bag in disgust? No further debate is necessary—he sees and he lets go. Meditation works in a similar way, exposing our deepest beliefs to light and naturally causing us to let go of the false ones.

For any activity related to human society, compassion and love are vital, whether one is a politician, businessperson, scientist, engineer, or anything else. If such people carry out their professional work with a good motivation, that work becomes an instrument for human benefit. On the other hand, if people work at their profession out of selfishness or anger, the profession becomes distorted. Instead of bringing benefit for humankind, the knowledge gained in the profession brings disaster. Compassion is essential.

MAY 2

Compassion is the willingness to play in the field of dreams even though you are awake.

Every minute you perform hundreds of karmic actions, yet you are hardly conscious of any of them. In the stillness of meditation, however, you can listen to your mind, the source of all this activity. You learn to be aware of your actions to a far greater extent than ever before. This self-awareness leads to self-control, enabling you to master your karma rather than be mastered by it.

LAMA THUBTEN YESHE, IN *WISDOM ENERGY*

Mindfulness is never boring.

Within the limitations of the human form, we can't understand the nature of existence from the universal position of an All-Seeing God, with a macrocosmic view. What we can do is observe existence close-up, without judgment.

The experience of nirvana is beyond the scope of human concepts, including our reified ideas of existence and nonexistence.

People must realize that even with all these comforts, all this money, and a GNP that increases every year, they are still not happy. They need to understand that the real culprits are our unceasing desires. Our wants have no end.

MAY 8

Compassion is the best healer.

One Tibetan analogy notes that when a clean cloth is placed over a dung heap, it will gradually come to smell like dung, while another cloth placed over incense will come to smell very nice. Similarly, the environment in which practitioners (particularly those who are not yet highly realized) place themselves can have a powerful impact on their minds.

LORNE LADNER, *WHEEL OF GREAT COMPASSION*

Overcoming attachment does not mean becoming cold and indifferent. On the contrary, it means learning to have relaxed control over our mind through understanding the real causes of happiness and fulfillment, and this enables us to enjoy life more and suffer less.

Just as fog is dispelled by the strength of the sun
and is dispelled no other way,
preconception is cleared by the strength of realization.
There's no other way of clearing preconceptions.
Experience them as baseless dreams.
Experience them as ephemeral bubbles.
Experience them as insubstantial rainbows.
Experience them as indivisible space.

MILAREPA, *DRINKING THE MOUNTAIN STREAM*

VISITING WITH BUDDHIST MONK WU-K'O
AT HIS REMOTE DWELLING

Ever since your
residence here,
our visits together
have been few.

With the long rains,
the vegetable garden goes untended;
distant mountains shine
in autumn pools.

Withered leaves fall
on your inkstone;
broken clouds
float above your pillow.

A rude guest,
and a future Ch'an Master;
it's not fair
that I cling to our meetings.

A peaceful mind is a compassionate mind.

A monk asked, "All of the buddhas and all of
the buddhadharmas come forth from this sutra.
What is this sutra?"
Qinshan said, "Forever turning."

A devata said:
"One who has sons delights in sons,
One with cattle delights in cattle.
Acquisitions truly are a man's delight;
Without acquisitions one does not delight."

The Buddha answered:
"One who has sons sorrows over sons,
One with cattle sorrows over cattle.
Acquisitions truly are a man's sorrows;
Without acquisitions one does not sorrow."

When everything is clean-clear in your own mind,
nobody can create obstacles for you.

Life continues to create itself and fall away, and suffering returns, and delight arrives, if even for a moment—agony, peace, rapture.

MAY 18

It's no mystery that thinking can make us happy or miserable. Let's say you're sitting under a tree one fine spring day. Nothing particular is happening to you, except perhaps the breeze is ruffling your hair, yet in your mind you're far away. Maybe you're remembering another spring day several years back when you were feeling terrible. You had just lost your job, or failed an exam, or your cat had wandered off. That memory turns into a worry. "What if I lose my job again? Why did I ever say such-and-such to so-and-so? No doubt this or that will happen, and I'll be out on my ear. Now I'm really in for it! How will I pay my bills?" One worry brings up another, which brings up yet another. Soon you feel your life is in shambles—but all this while you've been sitting under the tree!

An act of meditation is actually an act of faith—of faith in your spirit, in your own potential. Faith is the basis of meditation. Not of faith in something outside you—a metaphysical buddha, an unattainable ideal, or someone else's words. The faith is in yourself, in your own "buddha-nature." You too can be a buddha, an awakened being that lives and responds in a wise, creative, and compassionate way.

Half the spiritual life consists in remembering what we are up against and where we are going.

All those who have a role to play in finance and business should develop a sense of responsibility based on altruism and consider what is good for the entire world.

Having slain anger, one sleeps soundly;
Having slain anger, one does not sorrow;
The killing of anger,
With its poisoned root and honeyed tip:
This is the killing the noble ones praise,
For having slain that, one does not sorrow.

We confuse attachment with love. Attachment is concerned with *my* needs, *my* happiness, while love is an unselfish attitude, concerned with the needs and happiness of others. Most of the time our love is mixed with attachment because we do not feel adequate or secure on our own, and try to find wholeness through another. We become dependent on the good feelings and comfort of the relationship and then suffer when it changes. A relationship free of unrealistic grasping is free of disappointment, conflict, jealousy, and other problems, and is fertile ground for the growth of love and wisdom.

Generosity begins with our recognition of our debt to others.

With the proper understanding of transformation, whatever we do, twenty-four hours a day, can bring us closer to our goal of totality and self-fulfillment. All our actions—walking, eating, and even urinating!—can be brought into our spiritual path. Even our sleep, which is usually spent in the darkness of unconsciousness or in the chaos of dreams, can be turned into the clear-light experience of subtle, penetrating wisdom.

WHILE TRAVELING

With so much on my mind,
it's hard to express myself in letters.

How long has it been since I left home?
Old friends are no longer young.

Frosted leaves fall into empty bird nests;
river fireflies weave through open windows.

I stop at a forest monk's,
and spend the night in "quiet sitting."

When someone asks you a question, answer him or her sincerely, and when you are not asked, do not force your teaching upon others.

When you see a truck bearing down on you, by all means jump out of the way. But spend some time in meditation, too. Learning to deal with discomfort is the only way you'll be ready to handle the truck you didn't see.

MAY 29

Although we all have the sense of having a mind and of existing, our understanding of our mind and how we exist is generally vague and confused. We rightly say, "I have a mind or consciousness," "I am," "I exist"; we identify ourselves with a "me," an "I" to which we attribute qualities. But we do not know the nature of this mind, or of this "me." We do not know what they consist of, how they function, or who or what we really are.

In order to recognize our self-image, we can no longer identify with it. In other words, we have to learn how to objectify our own mental processes.

MAY 31

Don't cling to anything and don't reject anything. Let come what comes, and accommodate yourself to that, whatever it is. If good mental images arise, that is fine. If bad mental images arise, that is fine, too. Look on all of it as equal, and make yourself comfortable with whatever happens. Don't fight with what you experience, just observe it all mindfully.

Buddha isn't found by searching.
Look at the characteristic of your mind.

Whether we sit with our arms folded this way and our legs crossed that way is of little consequence. But it is extremely important to check and see if whatever meditation we do is an actual remedy for our suffering.

LAMA THUBTEN YESHE, IN *WISDOM ENERGY*

JUNE 3

It is often thought that the Buddha's doctrine teaches us that suffering will disappear if one has meditated long enough, or if one sees everything differently. It is not that at all. Suffering isn't going to go away; the one who suffers is going to go away.

Human intelligence is the source of our problems. But it would be foolish to think that the solution is to reduce intelligence. There is only one way out: we must not let our intelligence be guided by negative and harmful emotions. It must be guided only by proper and positive motivation if it is to become marvelously constructive.

Skillful speech not only means that we pay attention to the words we speak and to their tone but also requires that our words reflect compassion and concern for others and that they help and heal, rather than wound and destroy.

Just as material things are made of dust, so too are our perceptions and thoughts mere dust. Just as it takes only a moment to wipe the dust from the surface of a mirror, so it takes only a moment to become enlightened; the moment all defiled intentions are cleared from our consciousness, we will see ourselves in the mirror of perfect truth.

MASTER HSING YUN, *DESCRIBING THE INDESCRIBABLE*

How much of your life do you spend looking forward to being somewhere else?

Suppose, friend, a black ox and a white ox were yoked together
by a single harness. Would one be speaking rightly if one were
to say: "The black ox is the fetter of the white ox; the white ox is
the fetter of the black ox"?

No, friend. The black ox is not the fetter of the white ox nor is
the white ox the fetter of the black ox, but rather the single harness
by which the two are yoked together: that is the fetter there.

So too, friend, the eye is not the fetter of forms, nor are mental
phenomena the fetter of the mind, but rather the desire and lust
that arise there in dependence on both: that is the fetter there.

JUNE 9

SEEKING BUT NOT FINDING
THE RECLUSE

Under pines
I ask the boy;

he says: "My master's gone
to gather herbs.

I only know
he's on this mountain,

but the clouds are too deep
to know where."

It is very important that you do not compare your actions to your partner's or judge your partner's behavior as unskillful. Rather, focus on your own actions and take responsibility for them. Recall those times when you looked into your partner's eyes and saw the pain you caused. Remind yourself that you have caused this person you love to suffer. If you can admit your own faults, if you can see how hurtful your actions were and tap into a sense of concern for your partner's well-being, then compassion and loving-friendliness will flow.

Caoshan asked Venerable Qiang, "The true body of Buddha is
like vast emptiness. When a thing appears there, it is like the
moon reflected in water. How would you express this
teaching?"

Qiang said, "It's like a donkey looking into a well."

Caoshan said, "You've said a lot, but you've only gotten eighty
percent of it."

Qiang said, "What would you say, Master?"

Caoshan said, "It's like the well looking at the donkey."

"Suppose, bhikkhus, people were to carry off the grass, sticks, branches, and foliage in this Jeta's Grove, or to burn them, or to do with them as they wish. Would you think: 'People are carrying us off, or burning us, or doing with us as they wish'?"

"No, venerable sir. For what reason? Because, venerable sir, that is neither our self nor what belongs to our self."

"So too, bhikkhus, the eye is not yours. Whatever feeling arises with mind-contact as condition, that too is not yours: abandon it. When you have abandoned it, that will lead to your welfare and happiness."

Dharma that's done is destroyed from without.
Dharma that happens dawns from within.

Everything is as it is. It has no name other than the name we give it. It is we who call it something; we give it a value. We say this thing is good or it's bad, but in itself, the thing is only as it is. It's not absolute; it's just as it is. People are just as they are.

JUNE 15

Though becoming a monk or a nun is indeed one way of practicing generosity, most people can let go in the midst of busy, family-centered lives. What we need to reject is not the things we have, or our family and friends, but rather our mistaken sense that these are our possessions. We need to let go of our habit of clinging to the people and the material things in our lives and to our ideas, beliefs, and opinions.

Like a reflection in the mirror—
apparent yet insubstantial—
deity makes offerings to deities.
Reality sports in the field of reality,
and on the state of freedom from addiction to concepts
I impress the seal of impartial dedication.
That's my way of dedicating food.

Unless we have the determination to increase our mindfulness from moment to moment, we will easily forget to practice it.

Most people don't seem to realize how crucial real marriage is. Mad love is not enough. In a real marriage, the couple should base their love not just on attraction but also on mutual understanding and genuine respect, rooted in an appreciation of each other's qualities. A sense of commitment and responsibility will naturally follow.

HIS HOLINESS THE DALAI LAMA, *IMAGINE ALL THE PEOPLE*

JUNE 19

While practicing generosity, we should always remember
how very fortunate we are to have this opportunity.

JUNE 20

Mind can be compared to an ocean, and momentary mental events such as happiness, irritation, fantasies, and boredom to the waves that rise and fall on its surface. Just as the waves can subside to reveal the stillness of the ocean's depths, so too is it possible to calm the turbulence of our mind to reveal its natural pristine clarity.

With all this talk of non–self-existence and the illusory nature of phenomena we might conclude that ourselves, others, the world, and enlightenment are totally non-existent. Such a conclusion is nihilistic and too extreme. Phenomena do exist. It is their apparently concrete and independent *manner* of existence that is mistaken and must be rejected.

Take the example of a rainbow. Does it exist or not? Of course it does, but how? As something arising from the interplay of droplets of water in the sky, sunlight, and our own point of observation. A rainbow, then, is an *interdependent* phenomenon, and if we investigate, we can discover its various causes and conditions.

In a similar way, all existent phenomena are mere appearances to the mind; lacking concrete self-existence, they come into being from the interplay of various causes and conditions. This is true of ourselves as well. We and all other phenomena without exception are empty of even the smallest atom of self-existence, and it is this *emptiness* that is the ultimate nature of everything that exists.

We should surrender our intention to selfishly seek merit and recognition for our merit, and instead simply plant merit and cultivate wisdom.

LATE IN THE DAY,
GAZING OUT FROM A RIVER PAVILION

Water to the horizon
veils the base of clouds;
mountain mist
blurs the far village.

Returning to nest, birds
make tracks in the sand;
passing on the river, a boat
leaves no trace on the waves.

I gaze at the water
and know its gentle nature;
watch the mountains
until my spirit tires.

Though not yet ready
to leave off musing,
dusk falls,
and I return by horse.

When it is impossible for anger to arise within you, you find no outside enemies anywhere. An outside enemy exists only if there is anger inside.

Don't think. See.

Transforming appearances is easy;
keeping it to the end is hard.

ADEPT GODRAKPA, IN *HERMIT OF GO CLIFFS*

What Kwan Yin most clearly embodies is the quality of compassion. She is called "She Who Hears the Cries of the World" and steps forward to help all suffering beings. Meditating on Kwan Yin—as she sits by the river holding a willow branch, or as she stands on a lotus blossom holding her vial containing the elixir of compassion to pour out over the world—can soften our hearts and open us to the truth of our sharing with all beings, human and otherwise, in our living. She asks us to listen, as she does, to the cries of the world, and to begin always by sending compassionate caring to ourselves.

SANDY BOUCHER, *HIDDEN SPRING* 179

If you can cultivate wholesome mental states prior to sleep and allow them to continue right into sleep without getting distracted, then sleep itself becomes wholesome.

HIS HOLINESS THE DALAI LAMA, *SLEEPING, DREAMING, AND DYING*

The pleasure and joy that arise in dependence on the eye: this is the gratification in the eye. That the eye is impermanent, suffering, and subject to change: this is the danger in the eye. The removal and abandonment of desire and lust from the eye: this is the escape from the eye.

Actions motivated by attachment, aversion, or ignorance, regardless of any external appearances, are simply not Buddhist practices.

Pain is inevitable, suffering is not.

JULY 2

From contact comes feeling. From feeling comes reaction. This is what keeps us in the cycle of birth and death. Our reactions to our feelings are our passport to rebirth.

JULY 3

In Buddhism, the essential meaning of the word "study" is the unceasing, dedicated observation and investigation of whatever arises in the mind, be it pleasant or unpleasant. Only those familiar with the observation of mind can really understand Dharma.

JULY 4

For me, the indication that something is really wrong with today's world is that when the United States' economy sneezes, the whole world catches a cold.

Although you may understand the explanations, if you are still suffering because of problems, you clearly do not understand the true nature of your mind, your body, and your senses.

Suffering chastens us and makes us remember. We are like
the child who tries to pick up fire and is unlikely to do it again,
once she has seen the consequences. With material things,
seeing is easy; but when it comes to picking up the fires of greed,
aversion, and delusion, most of us aren't even aware we're
holding fires at all. On the contrary, we misguidedly believe
them to be lovable and desirable, and so we are never chastened.
We never learn our lesson.

JULY 7

Happy is one who knows samsara and nirvana are not two.

Intention is the core of all conscious life. It is our intentions that create karma, our intentions that help others, our intentions that lead us away from the delusions of individuality toward the immutable verities of enlightened awareness. Conscious intention colors and moves everything.

Unlike grass, which can be wiped out in a strong wind, we are as the earth.

JULY 10

The happiness we seek, a genuine lasting peace and happiness, can be attained only through the purification of our minds. This is possible if we cut the root cause of all suffering and misery—our fundamental ignorance.

HIS HOLINESS THE DALAI LAMA, *THE WORLD OF TIBETAN BUDDHISM*

Adverse circumstances test our courage, our strength of mind, and the depth of our conviction in the Dharma. There is nothing exceptional about practicing Dharma in a good environment and atmosphere. The true test is if we can maintain our practice in adverse conditions.

When we give food to a group of beggars, it would not be right to give food to some and not to others, since all are equal in their hunger and need for food. Similarly, we and all other sentient beings completely lack uncontaminated happiness and do not even experience perfect contaminated happiness. Since we are all equal in lacking happiness, although constantly wishing to obtain it, it would not be right to wish to give happiness to some and not to others. We should wish to benefit all sentient beings equally.

If happiness hasn't been recognized when alone,
a group of many people will be a cause of distraction.

To be attached to one's own happiness
is a barrier to the true and perfect path.
To cherish others is the source
of every admirable quality known.

TSONGKHAPA, *THE SPLENDOR OF AN AUTUMN MOON*

Mindfulness is not just a word or a discourse by the Buddha, but a meaningful state of mind. It means we have to be here now, in this very moment, and we have to know what is happening internally and externally. It means being alert to our motives and learning to change unwholesome thoughts and emotions into wholesome ones. Mindfulness is a mental activity that in due course eliminates all suffering.

A monk asked Master Bajiao, "Without asking about principles or points of discussion, I invite the master to point directly at the original face."

Master Bajiao sat upright, silently.

Anything that acts as an antidote to self-grasping is Dharma practice. Whereas, even though we may engage in a great variety of practices that may appear to be spiritual, if they do not act to destroy our self-grasping, they are not Dharma practice.

If we single-pointedly practice great compassion, then, with little effort, we will be able to gain all other virtues.

Resounding with a host of nymphs,
Haunted by a host of demons!
This grove is to be called "Deluding":
How does one escape from it?

"The straight way" that path is called,
And "fearless" is its destination.
The chariot is called "unrattling,"
Fitted with wheels of wholesome states.

The sense of shame is its leaning board,
Mindfulness its upholstery;
I call the Dharma the charioteer,
With right view running out in front.

One who has such a vehicle—
Whether a woman or a man—
Has, by means of this vehicle,
Drawn close to Nirvana.

The Buddha's teaching on causes and their results makes clear that accepting responsibility for our actions is the foundation for personal well-being and fulfillment. Denying your shortcomings and blaming the world for your discontent keeps you mired in unhappiness. Bad things happen to everyone. As long as you blame your parents or society for your problems, you give yourself an excuse not to change. The moment you accept responsibility for your situation, even though others may have contributed to it, you begin to move in a positive direction.

See everyone as a Buddha. This purifies the mind of ignorance and arrogance.

In the beginning mindfulness takes away worries and fears about past and future and keeps us anchored in the present. In the end it points to right view of the self.

Driven on by the profound, great iron goad
of strongly motivated good wishes,
I look again and again at basic reality
with gentle, undistracted cultivation
free from hope and from despair.

The ultimate source of peace in the family, the country, and the world is altruism.

The essence of our experience is change. Change is incessant. Moment by moment life flows by and it is never the same. Perpetual alternation is the essence of the perceptual universe. A thought springs up in your head and half a second later, it is gone. In comes another one, and that is gone too. A sound strikes your ears, and then silence. Open your eyes and the world pours in, blink and it is gone too. People come into your life and they leave again. Friends go, relatives die. Your fortunes go up, and they go down. Sometimes you win and just as often you lose. It is incessant: change, change, change.

Tibetan lamas often say: "Not seeing is the perfect seeing." Strange words, perhaps, but they have a profound meaning. They describe the advanced meditator's experience of spacious, universal reality, the experience beyond dualism.

LAMA THUBTEN YESHE, *INTRODUCTION TO TANTRA*

JULY 27

Inner refuge is refuge in ourselves, in our ultimate potential. When we recognize and nourish this potential, we have found the real meaning of refuge.

LITTLE PINES

Poking up from the ground barely above my knees,
already there's holiness in their coiled roots.
Though harsh frost has whitened the hundred grasses,
deep in the courtyard, one grove of green!

In the late night long-legged spiders stir;
crickets are calling from the empty stairs.
A thousand years from now who will stroll
    among these trees,
fashioning poems on their ancient dragon shapes?

JULY 29

If we do not try, we will not know.

Reality is like a face reflected in the blade of a knife; its properties depend on the angle from which we view it.

MASTER HSING YUN, *DESCRIBING THE INDESCRIBABLE*

Adopting the practice of generosity and loving-friendliness one day a week or once a month or once a year or periodically is not enough. We should practice these virtues throughout our lives in order to help ourselves and others have peace. These practices are not restricted to saints, far and above the hearts and minds of human beings. These practices are the guidelines for peaceful living among ordinary people.

About the nature of reality I cannot speak—
an artist without hands
draws pictures in the sky,
without eyes sees myriad things
in perfect vision without movement or strain.

Let go. Learn to flow with all the changes that come up. Loosen up and relax.

Desire and hatred, fear and folly:
He who breaks the law through these,
Loses all his fair repute
Like the moon at waning-time.

Desire and hatred, fear and folly,
He who never yields to these
Grows in goodness and repute
Like the moon at waxing-time.

BUDDHA, IN *THE LONG DISCOURSES OF THE BUDDHA*

A monk asked, "If on the road one meets a person of the
Way, how could one respond to that person with neither
words nor silence?"
Daopi said, "With kicks and punches."

We must admit the fact that there are things wrong with us—defilements, imperfections, hindrances—that no amount of rationalization or self-affirmation will cure, and that, left in place, will continue to pain us and deprive us of peace. When, therefore, we turn to religion for relief from hurt, fear, and confusion, we need more than tremulous hopes for our own betterment. We need a calm, unbiased vision of what is actually happening when we intend and act.

It is best not to silence the mind with a crushing blow of our will.

Look at children. Of course they may quarrel, but generally speaking they do not harbor ill feelings as much or as long as adults do. Most adults have the advantage of education over children, but what is the use of an education if they show a big smile while hiding negative feelings deep inside? Children don't usually act in such a manner. If they feel angry with someone, they express it, and then it is finished. They can still play with that person the following day.

Never strike at the heart.

AUGUST 9

Fools are happy when acquiring wealth;
noble people find happiness in giving it all away.
Lepers feel better when they scratch their sores,
but note how the wise dread leprosy.

SAKYA PANDITA, IN *ORDINARY WISDOM*

AUGUST 10

Everything comes to pass, nothing comes to stay.

Like clouds disappearing into the sky,
cognition absorbs into emptiness' sphere.

AUGUST 12

One day one of the Brahmins who objected to the Buddha
came to listen to one of the Buddha's discourses and, while
he was still speaking, walked up and down in front of him.
Then he proceeded to abuse the Buddha, using quite rough
language. He reviled him in every possible way he could think
of. When he had finally run out of words the Buddha, who
had been quietly sitting there listening, said, "Brahmin, do
you ever have guests in your house?" The Brahmin answered,
"Yes, of course we have guests in our house." The Buddha said,
"When you have guests in your house, do you offer them
hospitality? Do you offer them food and drink?" The Brahmin
said, "Well, of course we do. Of course I offer them food and
drink." The Buddha continued, "And if they don't accept your
hospitality, if they don't take your food and drink, to whom
does it belong?" The Brahmin said, "It belongs to me.
It belongs to me." The Buddha said, "That's right, Brahmin.
It belongs to you."

This is a good story to remember. Any abuse, anger, or threat
belongs to the one who is uttering it. We don't have to accept it.

I have not abandoned what is directly visible, friend, in order to pursue what takes time. I have abandoned what takes time in order to pursue what is directly visible. For the Blessed One has stated that sensual pleasures are time-consuming, full of suffering, full of despair, and the danger in them is still greater, while this Dharma is directly visible, immediate, inviting one to come and see, applicable, to be personally experienced by the wise.

Zen master Changqing Huileng entered the hall to address the monks. After a long silence he said, "Don't say that it will be any better tonight." He then got down and left the hall.

Our mind and our delusions are formless and colorless. However, our ignorance believing in true existence is harder than a rocky mountain. Our delusions are harder than steel.

AUGUST 16

When we are dying, we cannot turn around and go back toward health. Dying requires that we take the step without proof. We walk through the door. We cannot turn around and go back, so we walk through. The end. No guarantees, no certainty, no assurance. We walk, taking each step not from fear but from love, because a great mystery is blessing each footfall. Our hearts understand that mystery and feel the joy. It is the mystery returning to itself.

Whatever attitudes we habitually use toward ourselves, we will use on others, and whatever attitudes we habitually use toward others, we will use on ourselves. The situation is comparable to our serving food to ourselves and to other people from the same bowl. Everyone ends up eating the same thing—we must examine carefully what we are dishing out.

Phenomena of superficial samsara
don't exist—yet appear! Great wonder!

We should always remember that meditation is the cultivation and practice of nonattachment. The Buddha taught only the middle way, and mindfulness is nothing but the middle way. It is neither an intense practice, nor can it be done without effort. It must be done with balance. Properly done, it is neither detached pushing away nor egoistic clinging. Be very careful about sitting down with ideas like, "I am sitting, I am watching, I am breathing, I am meditating, I am this, that is mine."

Realizations come naturally through the practice of surrendering.

There is a current tendency among Dharma practitioners to be too eager to attend initiations given by any lama without any critical investigation. Afterwards, when things do not work out well, they easily speak badly of the lama. This, I think, is not a good habit.

Fulfillment of desire is an illusion; desire leads to more desire, not satisfaction.

Learning is like a design in water,
contemplation like a design on the side of the wall,
meditation like a design in stone.

I learned zazen from living spiritual masters, sitting in the room with me, giving talks, interviewing me privately, and being my friends and companions; whereas I have only read about the Christian tradition of meditation. In no way at all could that reading have put me on the right track by itself. I needed a living teacher and a community to practice with.

HEARING THE GIBBONS CALL
IN PA GORGE

As I lean
On my oar, gazing
At the cloud-line, purity
Emerges, deep and lonely,
From the Gorge.

When the mind
Doesn't have anything
On it, there's no sorrow
Inherent in repeated calls. They bear
The dew where every peak is distant,
Dangle in space where a slice
Of Moon shines
Bright.

Whoever
Hears it like this
Can finish a poem
By dawn.

If we're looking for outer conditions to bring us contentment, we're looking in vain.

A mantra is not like a prayer to a divine being. Rather, the mantra is the deity, is enlightenment, immediately manifest.

LORNE LADNER, *WHEEL OF GREAT COMPASSION*

Buddha's teachings are so simple and straightforward. If you find them complicated, it is only because you have made them so. You may think, "I have a Ph.D. and have amassed all this knowledge, yet I still can't figure out how to begin practicing Dharma." The remedy is to take a good look at your own mind.

You can't ever get everything you want. It is impossible. Luckily,
there is another option: You can learn to control
your mind, to step outside of this endless cycle of desire
and aversion. You can learn not to want what you want,
to recognize desires but not be controlled by them.

Another shortcoming of desire is that it leads to so much that is undesirable.

Through developing wisdom we can achieve awakening.
The Buddhadharma is not about anything else; it is about
accomplishing and perfecting one's own character. When one
has perfected one's character, love and compassion will exist.
Without them, we will suffer from resentment, unhappiness,
and blame.

Every time a problem arises, the essential thing is to immediately become aware that the problem comes from our selfish mind, that it is created by self-cherishing thoughts. As long as you put the blame outside yourself, there can be no happiness.

We can be aware of an imperfection without making any problem about it. In other words, the mind becomes an embracing mind.

Our mind is like an onion, and each day and month of practice progressively peels away the layers of delusion.

We meet
to part again.
I have no words to respond
to this double inspiration.

SEPTEMBER 5

All things are interrelated and interdependent; nothing exists in isolation. The entire universe is one ecosystem, similar to a spider web—if one part is touched, the entire net shimmers. As a result of interrelatedness and interdependency, every expression of energy, including our thoughts and intentions, ultimately touches and affects everything else.

SEPTEMBER 6

Meditation is running into reality. It does not insulate you from the pain of life. It allows you to delve so deeply into life and all its aspects that you pierce the pain barrier and go beyond suffering.

Some people think that having self-discipline prevents you from being open and natural. They think you should just relax and let everything flow freely. But to do so is not contradictory to being disciplined. In fact, you can be truly open only if you are disciplined.

SEPTEMBER 8

Flowing waters never return—save your sighs;
white clouds leave no trail—don't even try to chase them!
An idle man knows where to while away idleness:
yellow leaves, fresh breeze, a grove full of cicadas.

We're all being reborn at every moment. Look upon each morning as a rebirth and we may understand that only this one day exists. What will happen next time is completely dependent upon what we are doing now, therefore only "now" is important. "Now" is the cause; next life is the result.

A monk asked, "What is the monk's true eye?"
Xianglin said, "No separation."

Accept everything that arises. Accept your feelings, even the ones you wish you did not have. Accept your experiences, even the ones you hate. Don't condemn yourself for having human flaws and failings. Learn to see all the phenomena in the mind as being perfectly natural and understandable. Try to exercise a disinterested acceptance at all times with respect to everything you experience.

Happiness and suffering come from your own mind, not from outside. Your own mind is the cause of happiness; your own mind is the cause of suffering. To obtain happiness and pacify suffering, you have to work within your own mind.

Notice changes. If you do not inquire into your sensations, you might perceive them as unbearably intense, and presume they will continue to be so for a long time. However, if you do inquire into your sensations, you will soon notice their evanescent nature. Sensations differ from second to second; they might disappear entirely within minutes. The realizations that sensations come and go will allow you to break your tendency to "permanentize" and assume that things are more lasting and painful than they ever could be.

If the generally accepted concept were to obtain what we really need and then be content, society would be completely different. We would not be always tortured by fear and anxiety. We could just relax and be happy. Developing a sense of contentment is a precious gift.

SEPTEMBER 15

This robe of freedom from cold
isn't matched by ordinary clothes.

This concentration free of hunger
is unequaled by ordinary meat and beer.

This draught at the stream of enlightenment
isn't matched by ordinary drink.

This satisfaction born within
isn't equaled by ordinary treasure.

Every day we have an opportunity to learn, as there is hardly a human being without some daily *dukkha*.

A devata asked:
"What is good until old age?
What is good when established?
What is the precious gem of humans?
What is hard for thieves to steal?"

Buddha answered:
"Virtue is good until old age;
Faith is good when established;
Wisdom is the precious gem of humans;
Merit is hard for thieves to steal."

SEPTEMBER 18

Adopting an attitude of universal responsibility is essentially
a personal matter. The real test of compassion is not what
we say in abstract discussions but how we conduct ourselves
in daily life.

SEPTEMBER 19

Relying on solitude is easy;
giving up things to do is hard.

We can compare positive states of mind to water at rest
and deluded states of mind to turbulent, boiling water.
If we investigate the nature of the boiling water, we will
discover that, despite the turbulence, each individual
droplet is still clear. The same is true of the mind: whether
it is calm or boiled into turbulence by the overwhelming
complexity of dualistic views, its basic nature remains
clear and conscious.

LAMA THUBTEN YESHE, *INTRODUCTION TO TANTRA*

SEPTEMBER 21

If we find our minds have become agitated, the antidote is to relax more deeply. Relax away the effort that is going into sustaining our conceptual or emotional turbulence.

There is a difference between watching the mind and controlling the mind. Watching the mind with a gentle, open attitude allows the mind to settle down and come to rest. Trying to control the mind, or trying to control the way that one's spiritual practice will unfold, just stirs up more agitation and suffering.

Sometimes the best we can do may be very good; sometimes it is only mediocre.

People who enlighten me are all my buddhas. Instead of trying to find buddhas in high and precious places, shouldn't you be able to find your buddhas in your town, in your marketplaces, and in your streets? Everyone has valuable and enlightening qualities. If you learned and practiced those qualities, it would be like meeting the Buddha and practicing his teachings.

Meditation is participatory observation. What you are looking at responds to the process of looking. What you are looking at is you, and what you see depends on how you look.

He who resorts to empty huts for lodging—
he is the sage, self-controlled.
He should live there, having relinquished all:
that is proper for one like him.

Though many creatures crawl about,
many terrors, flies, serpents,
the great sage gone to his empty hut
stirs not a hair because of them.

Though the sky might split, the earth quake,
and all creatures be stricken with terror,
though men brandish a dart at their breast,
the enlightened take no shelter in acquisitions.

Its essence is emptiness, so abandon self-denial and self-improvement. *Its* nature is empty radiance, so let your diligent effort drop away. Everything is unobstructed, so forget your preferences. Just as phenomena arise, let them be, and do not cling to them.

On the vast plain of emptiness
the wild beasts and bull yaks of thought circulate.

Breaking their pride with both dog and horse,
subduing them with both sword and spear,
I kill the wild beasts and bull yaks of thought.

The flesh is eaten in nonduality,
the taste experienced as great bliss.

If I go hunting, that's how I do it.

Life responds when we risk.

The important thing is to reflect. Reflect on yourself,
in your life. How are you living your life now? Is it terribly
complicated? How could you simplify it? Are you always prone
to looking for more, or to creating problems about
the way you happen to be living? Really be honest and look, and
ask yourself these questions. Try to use the practice of
meditation to help you with your reflection.

OCTOBER 1

Unless there is loving-kindness in our speech, it's going to come out wrong.

OCTOBER 2

Selflessness is the most subtle and difficult characteristic to observe. However, when we discover this characteristic for ourselves, we experience a sense of freedom that words cannot describe.

OCTOBER 3

Creative awareness lets you see the problems in your relationships clearly. We often relate to people only on certain conditions; we ask them to fulfill our needs or to be exactly as we want them to be. But the beauty of a relationship is that it enables you to open to another person, and that person to you. With creative awareness, you become more aware and appreciative of other people. You see them as they are, not as you want them to be. You recognize their good qualities but you also see their foibles and have space for those too: you begin to love them unconditionally. Acceptance is the ground of love.

OCTOBER 4

Be gentle with yourself. Be kind to yourself. You may not be perfect, but you are all you've got to work with. The process of becoming who you will be begins first with the total acceptance of who you are.

BHANTE HENEPOLA GUNARATANA, *MINDFULNESS IN PLAIN ENGLISH*

278

The world's end can never be reached
by means of traveling through the world,
Yet without reaching the world's end
there is no release from suffering.

Therefore, truly, the world-knower, the wise one,
gone to the world's end, fulfiller of the holy life,
having known the world's end, at peace,
longs not for this world or another.

Investigation and contemplation can be done at any time—
during meditation, while watching the ocean, or even while just
walking. Whenever the mind wants to turn to its true nature, it
will reflect upon it. I hope your heart is open to these words.

The correct motivation for every action is essential.

When Buddhists say, "A bodhisattva fears not the result, but only the cause," they mean that we must expend the bulk of our energy planting good roots today, rather than fretting about the plants that are already growing from the roots we planted in the past.

OCTOBER 9

The mind is like the wick of a lamp
illumined only through its own radiance.

There are too many things in this world to be learned, and life is too short to learn everything, so we should complete that which we have begun rather than dabbling in many things.

GESHE NGAWANG DHARGYEY, IN *ADVICE FROM A SPIRITUAL FRIEND*

OCTOBER 11

Physical death is a more dramatic manifestation of the dying that goes on continually throughout the day. We are perpetually facing the beginnings and endings of situations and circumstances without appreciating the emotional toll that these small births and deaths have on our lives. It can be as subtle as forgetting a thought or as common as falling asleep. Change itself is a death.

OCTOBER 12

The role of our conceptual projection is deeply ingrained, much of it occurring either unconsciously or only semiconsciously. Because conceptualization is largely semiconscious, we usually are not aware that this compulsive and semiconscious interpretation is taking place. Instead, we tend to assume we are not projecting anything on reality at all, and that our basic sense of things is valid. There can be a lot of delusion in that.

B. ALAN WALLACE, *TIBETAN BUDDHISM FROM THE GROUND UP*

Ignorance may be bliss, but it does not lead to liberation.

A monk asked, "What is Shouchu's sword?"
Shouchu said, "Why?"
The monk said, "This student wants to know."
Shouchu said, "Wrong!"

OCTOBER 15

If we don't begin with ourselves, we have no way of actually, truly loving others.

If one is lonely neither in a crowd nor in the deep mountains, one is an able person who knows how to enjoy absolute freedom.

OCTOBER 17

Every experience we have in our lives manifests from our mind. Because you interpret your life and your world through your mental attitude, it is important to have the right motivation.

When we are aware of correctness and are satisfied with it, when we feel proper and content, the heart is entertained and the mind is amused.

OCTOBER 19

The basis of Buddhist morality is that acting in unskillful ways leads to unhappy results, and acting in skillful ways leads to happy results. This simple principle of cause and effect is an aspect of what Buddhists call karma.

When you take refuge in the Buddha, Dharma, and Sangha, you commit yourself primarily to steadying your karma. The method for accomplishing this is meditation.

OCTOBER 21

Let us not talk of karma, but simply of our responsibility toward the whole world.

The five aggregates are truly burdens,
the burden-carrier is the person.
Taking up the burden is suffering in the world,
laying the burden down is blissful.

Having laid the heavy burden down
without taking up another burden,
having drawn out craving with its root,
one is free from hunger, fully quenched.

OCTOBER 23

Just imagine if we all lived with no compassion, thinking only of ourselves. We would suffer greatly. The more you think of others, the happier you are.

Since there's no end
to the desires of sentient beings,
all cannot be pleased.
Not thinking about the faults of others,
we must reduce our own worries instead.

The solution is not to suppress our thoughts and desires, for this would be impossible; it would be like trying to keep a pot of water from boiling by pressing down tightly on the lid. The only sensible approach is to train ourselves to observe our thoughts without following them. This deprives them of their compulsive energy and is therefore like removing the pot of boiling water from the fire.

It is difficult to imagine anything more inherently boring than sitting still for an hour with nothing to do but feel the air going in and out of your nose. You are going to run into boredom repeatedly in your meditation. Everybody does. Boredom is a mental state and should be treated as such.

Cold cliff
dead tree
this knobby-pated me
thinks there's nothing better than a poem.
I mock myself, writing
in the dust, and
damn the man who penned the first word
and steered so many astray.

Wanting to be somebody is dangerous. It is like playing with fire, and it hurts constantly. And other people will not play by our rules. People who really manage to be somebody, like heads of state, invariably need a bodyguard because they are in danger for their lives. When one is nobody and has nothing, there is peace.

OCTOBER 29

The key, during both life and death, is to recognize illusions as illusions, projections as projections, and fantasies as fantasies. In this way we become free.

In Buddhism, liberation is always *from* a state that needs healing and *to* a healed state of release and greater effectiveness. Buddha is viewed as like a physician; practitioners are like patients taking the medicine of Buddha's teaching in order to be cured from a basic illness and to achieve a state of health necessary for widely effective altruistic endeavor.

HIS HOLINESS THE DALAI LAMA, *KALACHAKRA TANTRA*

OCTOBER 31

Dying without fear takes a great deal of trust, a trust that can help us live with more faith, if we can understand our need to control. Death teaches us the power of letting be, of noninterference and surrender. The process of dying is completely natural. The laws of nature govern death as they do our lives. It is difficult to understand the power of not doing, of leaving these natural laws alone, when we have always attempted to act our own course. Death can teach us when to leave things alone and when to act.

A teacher is essential. If you went to buy a Rolls-Royce and instead got all the parts of the car and an instruction manual on how to assemble it, you'd panic: "What's this? Where's my car?" You would need someone to show you how to put it together. It's the same with meditation. We need someone to show us how to put everything together inside our minds.

While meditating, we are bound to find ourselves carried away by trains of thought. When we recognize this has happened, we may react with frustration, disappointment, or restlessness. All such responses are a waste of time.

A monk asked, "The mountains, the rivers, and the great earth—from where did all of these things come forth?"

Tiantai said, "From where did this question come forth?"

NOVEMBER 4

Seeing ourselves plainly, we can change, and as we do so,
it brings a feeling of great relief, as if we had dropped
a heavy load.

NOVEMBER 5

As *kusa* grass, wrongly grasped,
Only cuts one's hand,
So the ascetic life, wrongly taken up,
Drags one down to hell.

FROM *THE CONNECTED DISCOURSES OF THE BUDDHA*

The threshold between right and wrong is pain.

One day as I was meditating, I saw a rusty gutter, and I suddenly felt sad and sorry that it was going bad and rusty. I experienced that life was impermanent. I learned Dharma from that gutter.

MAE CHI BOONLIANG, IN *WOMEN'S BUDDHISM, BUDDHISM'S WOMEN*

NOVEMBER 8

When we see clearly, we can change.

Investigate yourself. Question everything. Take nothing for granted. Don't believe anything because it sounds wise and pious and some holy men said it. See for yourself. That does not mean that you should be cynical, impudent, or irreverent. It means you should be empirical. Subject all statements to the actual test of your own experience, and let the results be your guide to truth. Insight meditation evolves out of an inner longing to wake up to what is real and to gain liberating insight into the true structure of existence. The entire practice hinges upon this desire to be awake to the truth. Without it, the practice is superficial.

NOVEMBER 10

You can't negate negation
so how can being be?

You have to be careful not to criticize or fight the mind, since it is normal to think, hear sounds, and feel sensations. The trick is not to grasp or reject them. Just leave them alone and let them come and go lightly.

NOVEMBER 12

Nonattachment doesn't mean that you get rid of your spouse. It means you free yourself from wrong views about yourself and your spouse. Then you find that there's love there, but it's not attached. It's not distorting, clinging, and grasping. The empty mind is quite capable of caring about others and loving in the pure sense of love. But any attachment will always distort that.

The way the insubstantial sky appears
is that it may appear as anything.
The ceaseless insubstantial nature of mind
may also appear as anything.

The mind is the nucleus of samsara and nirvana.

Eventually we will find (mostly in retrospect, of course) that we can be very grateful to those people who have made life most difficult for us.

If you stay mindfully aware of the whole context of every interaction, you will also remember to be extra careful when you are vulnerable. If you are grieving the loss of someone or something you love, for instance, it may take less provocation to make you angry. You know, then, to be especially careful around other people, like a man without shoes walking softly where there may be glass. This is important, too, when you are ill, tired, hungry, lonely, in pain, or just plain grouchy. When you are under stress, moment-to-moment mindfulness helps you remember your vulnerability and avoid regrettable actions.

NOVEMBER 17

At the moment of enlightenment the concept of an experiencer who is having an experience totally dissolves. It is analogous to what would happen to a salt doll who jumped into the ocean to see what it was like; the doll would become one with the ocean that it was experiencing.

Desires achieved increase thirst like salt water.

Sometimes I say the buddhas and bodhisattvas are the most
selfish of all. Why? Because by cultivating altruism they achieve
ultimate happiness.

Bhikkhus, when ignorance is abandoned and true knowledge has arisen in a bhikkhu, then with the fading away of ignorance and the arising of true knowledge he no longer clings to sensual pleasures, no longer clings to views, no longer clings to rules and observances, no longer clings to a doctrine of self. When he does not cling, he is not agitated.

If we train our breathing, we can control our emotions—that is, we can cope with the happiness and pain in our lives. We should practice until we feel this; our practice is not complete until we can see this clearly.

BUDDHADASA BHIKKHU, *MINDFULNESS WITH BREATHING*

Shakyamuni Buddha said, "Judge not others; judge only yourself." What appear to be faults in others may actually be reflections of our own emotional afflictions.

If we have developed the necessary mental discipline and are sufficiently aware of what is happening inside us, there is no reason why we cannot choose to express only those thoughts that will bring happiness to ourselves and others. The whole world might rise against us, but if the ability to control our mind were well developed, we could still view everyone as our friend rather than cower with fear and hatred.

LAMA THUBTEN YESHE, IN *WISDOM ENERGY*

A hundred thousand worlds are flowers in the sky,
a single mind and body is moonlight on the water;
once the cunning ends and information stops,
at that moment there is no place for thought.

The best way to look at suffering is with gratitude, that it is happening in order to teach us some very important lesson. It is useless to want suffering to go away. It is impermanent, it will go away anyway, but if we don't learn the lesson that it is trying to teach us, it will come back in exactly the same manner.

A monk asked, "What is the ultimate teaching of all buddhas?"
Fayan said, "You have it too."

Mind is the basis of everything, of enlightenment as well as illusion.

The way out of a trap is to study the trap itself, learn how it is built. You do this by taking the thing apart piece by piece. The trap can't trap you if it has been taken to pieces. The result is freedom.

Treat others with the mind of giving, and practice doing works that have no reward.

The most valuable learning is not about memorizing facts and figures. It is not about higher grade point averages and accumulating degrees. It is about life itself, and its impact is on the heart.

Destruction of the nonexistent is easy;
no attachment to the existent is hard.

DECEMBER 2

Doubt is an insidious enemy—doubt in the Buddha, the Dharma, the Sangha, in the teacher, one's own abilities, the instructions, or even the whole concept of the teaching. These doubts make it not just hard but impossible to meditate. We have to let go of all that kind of thinking.

My basic feeling is that it is better for people to follow their own religious tradition. Maybe you realize that the Buddhist way is really more effective, but you must be absolutely certain this approach is for you. If you are sure, then you have the individual right to change. If you waver at all, it is better to follow your own tradition.

DECEMBER 4

You may be able to recite by heart and brilliantly explain teachings on emptiness. But in daily life, if someone says something a little negative or a little positive, offers a little criticism or a little praise, immediately the mind becomes emotional. There is no stability; immediately there is like and dislike. If this is what happens to our mind in daily life, there is not even a particle of practice of right view.

We must die to each moment and allow life to express itself through us. Our lives may not turn out the way in which the ego has imagined, but when we surrender to the truth of what is, we will find freedom beyond measure, as surely as the river finds its way to the sea.

DECEMBER 6

At the heart of Buddhist meditation are concentration and inquiry. When you cultivate these two qualities in meditation, you develop your ability to be quiet and clear, to offer understanding and love.

DECEMBER 7

View all problems as challenges. Look upon negativities that arise as opportunities to learn and to grow. Don't run from them, condemn yourself, or bury your burden in saintly silence. You have a problem? Great. More grist for the mill. Rejoice, dive in, and investigate.

BHANTE HENEPOLA GUNARATANA, *MINDFULNESS IN PLAIN ENGLISH*

SPENDING THE NIGHT
AT A VILLAGER'S PAVILION

The pillow for his bed
is a rock from mid-stream;

the spring from the well-bottom
flows to a pond through bamboo.

The night is half gone,
but the guest hasn't slept;

he alone hears
the mountain rain arrive.

Master Xinghua asked a monk, "Where are you coming from?"
The monk said, "From a precipitous Zen place."
Xinghua said, "Did you bring the shout of a precipitous
    Zen place?"
The monk said, "I didn't bring it."
Xinghua said, "Then you haven't come from there."
The monk shouted. Xinghua hit him.

DECEMBER 10

The Buddha is as near to you as your own heart.

To evaluate the degree of freedom that we might have at death, we can look at the degree of freedom we have right now. In terms of your daily life, how much freedom do you have? At nighttime while you're dreaming, how much freedom or control do you have during the dream-state? Just look at the degree of compulsive ideation or thoughts churning in the mind. If we don't have control over these, we can question the degree of control we will have when we enter into the transitional process.

Form is suffering. The cause and condition for the arising of form is also suffering. As form has originated from what is suffering, how could it be happiness?

What can we do to alleviate the suffering in the world? Pursuing this question may lead to great compassion, which is based on this sense of even-mindedness toward all living creatures. This is more than the wish "May you be free of suffering"; it is taking upon ourselves the task of alleviating the suffering of others, and of bringing others to a state of well-being.

DECEMBER 14

Loving others does not mean that we should forget ourselves.

When a noble disciple has thus understood the unwholesome
and the root of the unwholesome, the wholesome and the root
of the wholesome, he entirely abandons the underlying tendency
to lust, he abolishes the underlying tendency to aversion, he
extirpates the underlying tendency to the view and conceit
"I am," and by abandoning ignorance and arousing true
knowledge he here and now makes an end of suffering. In that
way too a noble disciple is one of right view, whose view is
straight, who has perfect confidence in the Dharma, and has
arrived at this true Dharma.

DECEMBER 16

Owning love is like trying to take possession of the air.

Meditation takes gumption. It is certainly a great deal easier just to sit back and watch television. So why bother? Why waste all that time and energy when you could be out enjoying yourself? Why? Simple. Because you are human. And just because of the simple fact that you are human, you find yourself heir to an inherent unsatisfactoriness in life, which simply will not go away. You can suppress it from your awareness for a time. You can distract yourself for hours on end, but it always comes back— usually when you least expect it. All of a sudden, seemingly out of the blue, you sit up, take stock, and realize your actual situation in life.

This going away
has no circumstantial cause;
a solitary cloud
just has no fixed home.

DECEMBER 19

When you have developed bodhichitta in your heart, all the good things in life are magnetically attracted to you and effortlessly pour down upon you like rain.

LAMA THUBTEN YESHE, *INTRODUCTION TO TANTRA*

The Buddha once asked one of his students, "What is the span of human life?"

The student answered, "It is a couple of days."

The Buddha said, "You do not know the practice yet."

The Buddha asked another student, "What is the span of human life?"

The student answered, "It is the time between meals."

The Buddha replied, "You also do not know the practice yet."

Again, he asked a different student, "What is the span of human life?"

The student answered, "It is the time between inhaling and exhaling."

The Buddha said, "You indeed know the practice."

Unconditional love is an expression of love that is not based upon pleasant feelings. It is instead unlimited. Anyone who meets an individual with unconditional love can experience its presence, and the one who expresses it becomes a loving person. It is similar to a flower that emits its fragrance without regard to the "worth" of those who smell it.

Moonlight and the sound of pines are things we all know,
Zen mind and delusion distinguish sage and fool.
Go back to the place where not one thought appears;
how shall I put this into words for you?

If we have said anything during the day that we now regret, we've lacked deliberation and lost mindfulness. There's no blame attached, only recognition.

Being in control suggests an attitude of individualism and self-sufficiency. It assumes an influence that is not typically borne out by experience. A need to control distances ourselves from others, and we experience a sterile aloneness, missing the connection and mutual support offered by relationships. We obstruct our connection with the spiritual.

Reality is like a priceless jewel, of which the most precious diamond is only an inadequate metaphor. Once the tar has been scraped away by meditation—layer after layer, meditation period after meditation period—then the jewel reveals itself. And we will see the freedom of this universe of pure existence just as it is —the Kingdom of Heaven.

TOM CHETWYND, *ZEN AND THE KINGDOM OF HEAVEN*

If one wants to achieve stature for oneself,
one must do only that which helps others.
Do not those who want to clean their faces
need first to wipe the mirror clean?

What you think is a problem comes from your own mind; what you think is joyful comes from your own mind. Your happiness does not depend on anything external.

LAMA ZOPA RINPOCHE, *TRANSFORMING PROBLEMS INTO HAPPINESS*

The Buddha compared being angry with picking up hot coals with bare hands and trying to throw them at one's enemy. Who gets burnt first? The one who's picking up the coals, of course—the one who is angry. We may not even hit the target we are aiming at, because if that person is clever and practiced enough, he'll duck—and we shall still have burnt hands.

When you are having a bad time, examine that badness, observe it mindfully, study the phenomenon, and learn its mechanics.

BHANTE HENEPOLA GUNARATANA, *MINDFULNESS IN PLAIN ENGLISH*

Zhaozhou asked a monk, "How many sutras do you read
in one day?"
The monk said, "Sometimes seven or eight. Sometimes ten."
Zhaozhou said, "Oh, then you can't read scriptures."
The monk said, "Master, how many do you read in a day?"
Zhaozhou said, "In one day I read one word."

A hundred thousand elephants,
A hundred thousand horses,
A hundred thousand mule-drawn chariots,
Are not worth a sixteenth part
Of a single step forward.

BUDDHA, IN *THE CONNECTED DISCOURSES OF THE BUDDHA*

BIBLIOGRAPHY

All the books from which *Daily Wisdom* is drawn are published
by Wisdom Publications.

Advice from a Spiritual Friend. Geshe Rabten and Geshe Ngawang
Dhargyey. 2001.

*Ama Adhe: The Voice That Remembers: The Heroic Story of a Woman's Fight
to Free Tibet.* Ama Adhe Tapontsang and Joy Blakeslee. 1997.

Awakening the Mind: Basic Buddhist Meditations. Geshe Namgyal
Wangchen. 1995.

Be an Island: The Buddhist Practice of Inner Peace. Ayya Khema. 1999.

*Becoming a Child of the Buddhas: A Simple Clarification of the Root Verses of
Seven-Point Mind Training.* Gomo Tulku. 1998.

Being Nobody, Going Nowhere: Meditations on the Buddhist Path. Ayya
Khema. 2001.

The Bliss of Inner Fire: Heart Practice of the Six Yogas of Naropa. Lama
Thubten Yeshe. 1998.

Buddhist Peacework: Creating Cultures of Peace. Ed. David W. Chappell.
2000.

The Clouds Should Know Me By Now: Buddhist Poet Monks of China.
Trans. Red Pine and Mike O'Connor. 1998.

*The Connected Discourses of the Buddha: A New Translation of the Samyutta
Nikaya.* Bhikkhu Bodhi. 2000.

Creation and Completion: Essential Points of Tantric Meditation. Jamgon Kongtrul. Trans. Sarah Harding. 1996.

Describing the Indescribable: A Commentary on the Diamond Sutra. Hsing Yun. 2001.

The Door to Satisfaction: The Heart Advice of a Tibetan Buddhist Master. Lama Zopa Rinpoche. 1994.

Drinking the Mountain Stream: Songs of Tibet's Beloved Saint, Milarepa. Milarepa. Trans. Brian Cutillo. 1995.

Eight Mindful Steps to Happiness: Walking the Buddha's Path. Bhante Henepola Gunaratana. 2001.

Everlasting Rain of Nectar: Purification Practice in Tibetan Buddhism. Geshe Jampa Gyatso. 1996.

The Flight of the Garuda: Teachings of the Dzokchen Tradition of Tibetan Buddhism. Keith Dowman. 1994.

The Good Heart: A Buddhist Perspective on the Teachings of Jesus. Tenzin Gyatso, His Holiness the Fourteenth Dalai Lama. 1996.

Heartwood of the Bodhi Tree: The Buddha's Teaching on Voidness. Buddhadasa Bhikkhu. 1994.

Hermit of Go Cliffs: Timeless Instructions from a Tibetan Mystic. Cyrus Stearns. 2000.

Hidden Spring: A Buddhist Woman Confronts Cancer. Sandy Boucher. 2000.

How to Meditate: A Practical Guide. Kathleen McDonald. 1994.

Imagine All the People: A Conversation with the Dalai Lama on Money, Politics, and Life As It Could Be. Tenzin Gyatso, His Holiness the Dalai Lama with Fabien Ouaki. 1999.

Introduction to Tantra: The Transformation of Desire. Lama Thubten Yeshe. 2001.

Journey to the Center: A Meditation Workbook. Matthew Flickstein. 1998.

Kalachakra Tantra: Rite of Initiation. Tenzin Gyatso, His Holiness the Fourteenth Dalai Lama. 1999.

Landscapes of Wonder: Discovering Buddhist Dhamma in the World Around Us. Bhikkhu Nyanasobhano. 1998.

Lessons from the Dying. Rodney Smith. 1998.

The Long Discourses of the Buddha: A New Translation of the Digha Nikaya. Maurice Walshe. 1995.

Luminous Mind: The Way of the Buddha. Kalu Rinpoche. 1996.

The Meaning of Life: From a Buddhist Perspective. Tenzin Gyatso, His Holiness the Fourteenth Dalai Lama. 1993.

Meditation for Life. Martine Batchelor. 2001.

The Middle Length Discourses of the Buddha: A New Translation of the Majjhima Nikaya. Bhikkhu Nanamoli and Bhikkhu Bodhi. 1995.

The Mind and the Way: Buddhist Reflections on Life. Ajahn Sumedho. 1995.

Mindfulness in Plain English. Bhante Henepola Gunaratana. 1994.

Mindfulness with Breathing: A Manual for Serious Beginners. Buddhadasa Bhikkhu. 1996.

Natural Liberation: Padmasambhava's Teachings in the Six Bardos. Padmasambhava. Ed. Gyatrul Rinpoche. 1997.

Opening the Eye of New Awareness. Tenzin Gyatso, His Holiness the Fourteenth Dalai Lama. 1999.

Ordinary Wisdom: Sakya Pandita's Treasury of Good Advice. Sakya Pandita. 2000.

Polishing the Diamond, Enlightening the Mind: Reflections of a Korean Buddhist Master. Jae Woong Kim. 1999.

Sleeping, Dreaming, and Dying: An Exploration of Consciousness. Tenzin Gyatso, His Holiness the Fourteenth Dalai Lama. 1997.

The Splendor of an Autumn Moon: The Devotional Verse of Tsongkhapa. Gavin Kilty. 2001.

Swallowing the River Ganges: A Practice Guide to the Path of Purification. Matthew Flickstein. 2001.

Tibetan Buddhism from the Ground Up: A Practical Approach for Modern Life. B. Alan Wallace. 1993.

Transforming Problems into Happiness. Lama Zopa Rinpoche. 2001.

Ultimate Healing: The Power of Compassion. Lama Zopa Rinpoche. 2001.

Wheel of Great Compassion: The Practice of the Prayer Wheel in Tibetan Buddhism. Ed. Lorne Ladner. 2000.

When I Find You Again, It Will Be in Mountains: The Selected Poems of Chia Tao. Trans. Mike O'Connor. 2000.

When the Iron Eagle Flies: Buddhism for the West. Ayya Khema. 2000.

Who Is My Self? A Guide to Buddhist Meditation. Ayya Khema. 1997.

Wisdom Energy: Basic Buddhist Teachings. Lama Thubten Yeshe and Lama Zopa Rinpoche. 2000.

Women's Buddhism, Buddhism's Women: Tradition, Revision, Renewal. Ed. Ellison Banks Findly. 2000.

The World of Tibetan Buddhism: An Overview of Its Philosophy and Practice. Tenzin Gyatso, His Holiness the Fourteenth Dalai Lama. 1995.

Zen and the Kingdom of Heaven: Reflections on the Tradition of Meditation in Christianity and Zen Buddhism. Tom Chetwynd. 2001.

Zen's Chinese Heritage: The Masters and Their Teachings. Andy Ferguson. 2000.

BHANTE GUNARATANA

EIGHT MINDFUL STEPS TO HAPPINESS:
Walking the Buddha's Path
288 pp., 0-86171-176-9, $16.95

The long-awaited sequel to the bestselling *Mindfulness in Plain English*. Here Bhante turns his unique and warm style toward the subject of the Noble Eightfold Path.

"Masterful."—Larry Rosenberg, author of *Breath by Breath*

Clear and straightforward."
—Joseph Goldstein, author of *Insight Meditation*

"Inspiration and encouragement to those truly interested in what it means to be happy."—Sharon Salzberg, author of *Lovingkindness*

MINDFULNESS IN PLAIN ENGLISH
208 pp., 0-86171-064-9, $14.95

An established favorite, which speaks like both an old friend and a teacher to newcomers and long-time meditators alike.

"A masterpiece. I cannot recommend it highly enough."
—Jon Kabat-Zinn, author of *Wherever You Go, There You Are*

"One of the best nuts-and-bolts meditation manuals. You can't do better." —Brian Bruya, Religion Editor, Amazon.com

AYYA KHEMA

BEING NOBODY, GOING NOWHERE:
Meditations on the Buddhist Path
Foreword by Zoketsu Norman Fischer
224 pp., 0-86171-198-X, $16.95

Winner of the Christmas Humphreys Award:
Best Introductory Buddhist Book

In this new edition of her classic bestseller, Ayya Khema gives clear, practical instruction for overcoming counterproductive habits and beliefs.

"To protestations of the difficulty of practice Ayya Khema always responded, 'It's simple, it's clear, you can do it. You can do it and when you do you will be grateful for it.' We are lucky to have her written teachings, which are so useful and so bracing. Through them her voice lives on."—Zoketsu Norman Fischer, Co-abbot, San Francisco Zen Center

BE AN ISLAND:
The Buddhist Practice of Inner Peace
Foreword by Sandy Boucher
160 pp., 0-86171-147-5, $14.95

"Real warmth of heart pervades these expositions, which in their directness and fresh immediacy also touch the heart of the reader."
—*The Middle Way: Journal of the Buddhist Society*

THE DALAI LAMA

THE GOOD HEART:

A Buddhist Perspective On The Teachings Of Jesus
224 pp., 0-86171-138-6, $14.95

"Arguably the best book on inter-religious dialogue published to date. One does not say such things lightly, but in a very real sense this is a holy book."—Huston Smith, author of *The Illustrated World's Religions*

IMAGINE ALL THE PEOPLE:

A Conversation with the Dalai Lama on Money, Politics, and Life As It Could Be
The Dalai Lama with Fabien Ouaki
192 pp., 0-86171-150-5, $14.95

If you could sit down with the Dalai Lama and talk about anything, what would you discuss? Here, in spontaneous, lively discussion, the Dalai Lama holds forth on money, politics, and life as it could be.

TRANSFORMING PROBLEMS INTO HAPPINESS

Foreword by His Holiness The Dalai Lama

104 pp., 0-86171-194-7, $12.95

"For anyone who needs to cope with life's problems. I recommend it very highly indeed." —Lillian Too, author of *The Complete Illustrated Guide to Feng Shui*

"Of great benefit."—His Holiness the Dalai Lama

ULTIMATE HEALING:

The Power of Compassion

Foreword by Lillian Too

288 pp., 0-86171-195-5, $16.95

Here Lama Zopa shows us that by developing compassion, we can eliminate the cause of all disease, and heal not only our bodies but our lives, and the world around us.

LAMA YESHE

INTRODUCTION TO TANTRA:

The Transformation of Desire
Edited by Jonathan Landaw ~ Foreword by Philip Glass
192 pp., 0-86171-162-9, $16.95

Tantra—so often misunderstood—is presented as
a practice leading to joy and self-discovery, with
a vision of reality that is simple, clear, and
relevant to our lives.

THE BLISS OF INNER FIRE

Heart Practice of the Six Yogas of Naropa
224 pp., 0-86171-136-X, $16.95

In this collection of his last major teachings, Lama
Yeshe illuminates the advanced practices for
Highest Yoga Tantra, inspiring us to discover for
ourselves our own capacity for inexhaustible bliss.

"Wisdom Publications has put out a wonderful series on Tibetan
Buddhism. *The Bliss of Inner Fire* is one of their best."
—*The Review of Arts, Literature, Philosophy, and the Humanities*